A Doula's Guide

to

Education

By Jemmais Keval-Baxter

The Ho'oponopono Doula™

Published by Matrilineal Ink

Matrilineal Ink

www.matrilineal.cl

Everything in this book is an expression of belief, faith, and opinion; it is not to be construed as medical advice. I am human, and I do make mistakes...frequently. In reading this book, you accept 100% responsibility for all of your actions (thoughts, words, and deeds) at all times.

Published by: Matrilineal Ink™

www.matrilineal.cl

ISBN: 978-1-9998071-7-7

A Doula's Guide

to

Education

By Jemmais Keval-Baxter

The Ho'oponopono Doula™

Published by Matrilineal Ink

Matrilineal Ink

www.matrilineal.cl

Other books in the series include:

A Doula's Guide to Nutrition
A Doula's Guide to The Placenta

A Doula's Guide to Breastfeeding

A Doula's Guide to Menstruation

Also by Jemmais Keval-Baxter
Ho'oponopono Birth: Meditations on
Ho'oponopono for Pregnancy and
Childbirth

Table of Contents

Introduction

Our children are constantly learning. Everything about the growing child and their developing brains are designed to absorb the world around them, find patterns and adapt their behavior. Even from the time in the womb, science clearly shows that children learn by repetition and respond to stimulus. In fact, a number of methods of in-utero education have been developed to stimulate the unborn child through exposure to sound, rhythm, music and the all-important conversations that each mother has with her fetus.

Many of these fetal education methods emphasize classical music such as Mozart and remind us that the mother's voice, which has the clearest resonance within the womb, is crucial to stimulating the intellect. These scientific studies have confirmed what most women and old-wives have advised for years, that it is possible to talk to your child, nurture your child and develop a relationship with them before they are born. It also confirms how great an influence the time that a child experiences in the womb has on his or her development, and that the emotions, nutrients, and social interactions of the mother while pregnant affect the child, positively or detrimentally.

Education is a lifelong process, no matter how old we are we can still learn from our mistakes, and the knowledge gained by accumulated experience is part of the great wealth of wisdom that our elders have to share with their families, communities, and societies. Every influence that a child is exposed to from its environment will shape it. The relationship that the child has with its family and their interactions with other members of the world will all contribute to forming the person that your child becomes.

Formal education is one of the most influential factors that contributes to the formation of man (and woman and society). The choices that we make about how we educate our children will affect them for the rest of their lives, and there is an extraordinary amount of pressure on us as parents to "get it right."

How you intend to educate your children is one of the major topics of discussion that I recommend to couples contemplating conception and during their pregnancy.

"It is easier to raise healthy children than fix broken adults" Teacher Stephen Ritz

Values

The first place to start and an area I feel is, unfortunately, missing from many concepts of education is to determine what priorities you really have for your child.

When I suggest making a list of priorities regarding the capacities that you hope your child will have, (which I do in fact recommend that you do, each parent individually, for later comparison), I am not just talking about, the ability to dance, or play the piano, read fluently and have excellent penmanship. Nor am I talking about your own personal ambitions for your child such as their following in your footsteps as a doctor or in the family business. What I am asking you to do, is consider what is truly important to your child for his or her future. What you want them to have to see them through every eventuality to prepare them to be parents themselves one day. Let me make some suggestions.

Physical Health

Physical health involves raising children on a nutritional sound diet of chemical free whole foods, educating them about nutrition, and encouraging them in healthy exercise, in whatever form inspires them, be it dance or yoga, a sport or martial art or simply running around in the park with their dog or a kite.

Happiness

Of course, everyone wants happiness, but how many of us really know what it means or where to find it. I am not talking about the happiness and joy that comes from fleeting pleasures like good food, watching sports or drinking a glass of wine. I am talking about the skills and capacities to be happy every day, to be satisfied with life, and to understand what truly matters, not the accumulation of wealth or any other unsatisfiable or perpetual search. A capacity to be happy, to be content, no matter what circumstances you find yourself in. Happiness is a capacity which can be cultivated within the individual and is not dependent upon external factors, comments or opinions. It may be worth examining if you have these skills yourself to impart to your children, or what you can do to discover and embody them for yourself.

Manners & Morals

Honor may be defined in different ways depending on the society in which you find yourself. A violent gang member's definition of honor may not be the same as a member of the church. Yet, we all follow codes of conduct that define acceptable behavior. If we teach our children well, then their sense of right and wrong will not be dependent upon the laws, societies or peer pressure which surrounds them, but by their own inner conscience. We hope to be able to trust our children to behave honorably, by our standards, whether we are there to observe them or not. We also want our children to be polite and well mannered, in order to demonstrate respect for themselves and the people around them.

Patience, Compassion, Honesty, Consideration & Positivity

There are so many other positive attributes that we wish our children to embody, some of them fall into the above category, but I add a couple of examples here to the list to make sure that they are not left out of yours. A positive, no problem attitude, no matter what the circumstances, can make an astounding difference. You must see the difference in attitude between a belligerent teenager complaining while doing their chores or homework compared with a conscientious adolescent contentedly getting on with their projects and duties.

Having a problem-solving "solution" attitude is one of the most critical factors when faced with an unpleasant task or an obstacle or challenge of any kind. Teaching your child to be positive, means demonstrating a positive attitude, children learn by experience and example. They won't just do what you say, they will do what you do. So be careful. Be the change you want to see in the world. Be the best man or woman that you can be, even if it takes effort (don't let them see the effort) so that your child can be the best they can be effortless.

Capacity

We want our children to be capable, regardless of their situation. Providing the practical life skills (combined with a positive "can do" attitude) in every area of life, is one of the greatest gifts that you can give. Formal education, and specialist classes and tutors can help to provide your child with expertise in areas that you are not so familiar with. I have seen many young men and women sent off to university by loving, overindulgent parents that wanted to do so much for their children that they sabotaged them. These children were so "well cared for" that they had no idea how to do their own washing, mending, and ironing, cook their own food, manage their own budget or survive by themselves. It is important to encourage capacity in your child. Children of a very young age will begin to demonstrate a longing for independence, and nothing makes a small (or big) child happier than learning to do something by themselves. They feel capable, powerful and safe because they can take care of themselves, even if they don't have to. This is one of the reasons that chores are so important to children, not for reward or remuneration, but to instill a particular capacity and an understanding of responsibility not just in caring for oneself but also in caring for others, and working as a team, within the family, community, and life in general.

Community

So much of community has been lost within modern society, families often work and play independently from one another rather than working together on common projects such as gardening, agriculture, harvesting, cooking, patchwork, woodwork, etc. Even less common is the sense of community with our neighbors that encourages us to work together and help one another. So many of our needs have been translated into commodities that were once fulfilled by the community, such as helping to raise a barn, caring for the sick and infirm, childcare (like looking after your neighbor's children for a few hours every so often). Instead, we have less personal contact and obligations with others because everyday needs are met by professionals to whom we pay money, rather than trade or exchange services. Bringing food to the family of a woman who has just given birth was once the obvious consideration of all her close family, friends and neighbors, they knew that she too would reciprocate when their time came. Yet, that sense of community has so often been lost. In work, unions once protected common rights, and people considered themselves part of a team, all striving under the same circumstances. Or, working in cooperation for communal benefits such as harvesting wild salmon and smoking it to be shared amongst the whole community throughout the following months. Today's society instead encourages competition.

Our school systems often instill the concept of competition in children from an early age. Teaching them to compete with one another for the best grade or the teacher's approval, society at large then feeds these fears and insecurities by competing women against one another in terms of beauty or academic achievement, and using these classifications to define personal worth and value. These measures make few winners, at the expense of many "losers." Ambitious young workers are encouraged to compete against one another to climb the ladder "of success." Teaching our children to care for others and to work well in a community and in a team, as well as in a family, is vitally important to their sense of well-being and security. No matter how brilliant anyone is, they can never be brilliant in isolation. Societies work together just as families work together, failing or thriving co-dependently. Elder siblings teach younger sibling the skills that they have learned, so that everyone is capable, and so that everyone can help.

Learning how to compromise, resolve conflict, negotiate, and work towards a shared resolution are key parts of a healthy community and a healthy society.

"In nature headlong growth and all-out competition are features of immature ecosystems, followed by complex inter-dependency, symbiosis, cooperation and the cycling of resources."

Sacred Economics: Money, Gift, and Society in the Age of Transition by Charles Eisenstein.

Self-Worth

The same school systems and societies which teach competition and try to use it to motivate children and adults to strive towards achievements also endanger the self-worth of the individual. The means of forcing people to strive and strive are based on the concept of instilling within the individual a belief that they are not good enough unless they are able to achieve whatever standard is held up before them. Therefore, many people develop eating disorders because they feel unworthy; because they do not reach an externally projected ideal of beauty. This is also why businessmen and academics who excel in their fields often find themselves dissatisfied in psychiatrist offices or self-medicating with alcohol, violence, and other substances. Because they feel that even though they have achieved all that they set out to, somehow there was no end to the nagging doubt from within themselves to prove their worth.

Proving worth to an external source, such as a teacher or a manager is a vital tool of the current paradigm of society, which sadly leaves people feeling empty, unable to validate themselves and constantly seeking validation from those around them. Imagine how vulnerable a teenager is to the pressure of his or her peers if (s)he seeks their approval and validation through drinking games, driving fast, violence, sexual promiscuity or drug taking or any of the other self-damaging activities that they are convinced will win them social approval. Even adults are not immune to such addictions, with powerful business people achieving their first million, then their first 10 million then their first billion, accumulating more wealth than they need to survive or even thrive in luxury. Yet never achieving "enough" because the external quantifications of success have not been able to fill the void of success left within them.

In Nourishing Traditions book of baby and childcare, the over attentive, excessively praising parent is considered detrimentally:

"While on the surface such parental behavior might seem to confer advantages on the child in the form of self-confidence and autonomy, unfortunately, the opposite often occurs. According to child psychologist Polly Young-Eisendrath, Ph.D., the child often becomes embedded in what she calls the "self-esteem trap," characterized by excessive self-consciousness, isolation, and relentless self-criticism. Instilling the premise that a child is "special" and "different" puts enormous pressure on the child at just the time when he wants most of all to be a part of a group, to be the same, not different from, his friends. The result of well-meaning praise may be the child who engages in constant attention seeking or the teenager who finds ways to dominate a scene by sulking and disengaging.... The greatest gift a parent can give a child is not the feeling of being "special," but the confidence of being normal. Such children very often surprise us with what they achieve as adults. "

If a child feels that they have worth and value aside from monetary gain, aside from popularity or beauty, if they can validate themselves, then they have a much better chance of achieving happiness, mental health, and success no matter what they end up doing with their lives.

Self-Discipline

It is necessary for every child to understand responsibility, to learn how to take care of their own needs and to contribute to the needs of others. However, it is one thing to do one's chores and homework, rise early, exercise and eat well in an environment which supports this routine, and quite another to maintain this level of discipline on one's own. Many children (and adults) have fallen astray when left to their own devices. Without the structure of a school, many children who have been indoctrinated to believe that they need to be taught to learn, fail to study for their own pleasure and interest. Many students sent off to university put on weight eating an unhealthy diet, and too many people finding themselves unemployed with an excess of pleasure time developing unhealthy habits, sleeping late, and watching TV or playing video games all day.

These may sound like unfair stereotypes, yet, they are realities for countless people, too depressed, lacking in energy, motivation and willpower to take responsibility for their own lives and their own futures. We often rely on external expectations, structures, routines and pressure to motivate us to do what we do. However, the most successful people, the most capable and admirable are those who find the inspiration, motivation, and self-discipline within themselves to work towards their goals when left to their own devices.

No matter what their environment and no matter what temptations may be found around them, they structure their own life and find the energy to achieve by themselves.

Encouraging children to develop self-discipline and sustain it throughout their young lives, ensures their capacity to continue to power themselves and achieve their own goals when they are inevitably allowed the freedom to organize their own lives in the future.

Resilience

No child is born afraid to fail. It takes months, years, for a child to sit up without support, walk, talk, drink from a cup and eat with a spoon. They fall, they miss their mouth, they make a mess, and they try again. Shame and humiliation are some of the most debilitating expressions of social anxiety that affect people, limiting their actions to only those which they feel will be successful due to fear of failure.

Yet, the most successful people in the world are those that know never to give up, to try and try and try again, because they have not finished until they have gotten it right. They understand that the only true way to fail is to give up. Every single one of us was born with that resilience, we were secure in the love of our parents, that it was acceptable for us to make mistakes and try again and get better. We were secure in ourselves knowing that failure was not a sign of weakness nor diminished our value but was merely a challenge that required determination and perseverance. What can we do to preserve that capacity? That self-motivation, faith, and resilience in our children, so that they can get up and try again no matter how many times they fall, or how badly they get hurt?

A Sense of Purpose

Without purpose. Life is meaningless and unfulfilling. Purpose drives us, fulfills us, inspires us and provides for us in every way possible.

"We are here to express our gifts; it is among our deepest desires, and we cannot be fully alive otherwise." **Sacred Economics: Money, Gift, and Society in the Age of Transition by Charles Eisenstein.**

"Plants know how to make food out of light and water. Not only ...feed themselves, but they make enough to sustain the lives of all the rest of us. Plants are providers for the rest of the community and exemplify the virtue of generosity."

Braiding Sweetgrass by Robin Wall-Zimmerman

Plants and animals are much simpler incarnations, plants are very pure, they are givers, they are the most productive, and the most creative, providing life for everything else on this planet. Most animals are very simple, their experiences on this earth are purposeful, the life that they are given defines their gifts and their responsibility, it is programmed into their form and their development, their instincts are undeniable.

Being born as a human provides the greatest challenge. Unlike other animals, a human is not born fully evolved, able to walk and respond to its environment in the same way as its parents. A newborn is defenseless, unable even to lift its own head. The greatest instinct of a newborn is to suckle, to live to survive, but from there we are an open book waiting for our experiences and environments to shape and form our characters and to write our stories.

Our plasticity as children makes us the most adaptable mammal on earth (bacteria and viruses seem to adapt at an equally fantastic rate). This has ensured our survival and provided for countless cultures whose very foundations have been based upon the resources they have available in their environment: from availability of foods, building materials, clothing, art, music, language, stories, and cosmo-visions based upon natural cycles such as seasonal weather patterns, even to the extent of activating different manifestations of our DNA. We are so greatly influenced and defined by the culture, society and environment that we are born into, that new generations are able to build upon the knowledge and abilities of past generations (for example, mobile phones were extremely uncommon when I was a child and non-existent when my parents where children, yet modern day infants absorb them as part of their culture, as the norm, and many learn to use technology at a very early age).

When a child is born, they absorb the life that saturates them (a baby born of Chinese descent growing up in a French-speaking household will learn to speak French first). We are not always able to follow a blueprint, a program for life, we are both blessed and cursed with the responsibility of making our own choices in life, of what to do and who to be, to seek out and discover our own purpose.

Society at large is motivated by an unsustainable consumerist, compulsion of greed, an insatiable hunger to want more. More: food, sex, alcohol, fitness, beauty, cars, power, money, gadgets, drugs, achievement. There is never a point at which we achieve satisfaction and fulfillment because following that model has no resolution, there is never enough.

So many people are lost, drowning in this corrupted mindset that they live the miracle of life as if it were mundane. The answer is to discover purpose and meaning that transcends existence for the sake of existence. To live without purpose is to navigate life without a compass or even a destination. Without purpose, millions of people become addicts to drugs that numb them from life, commit suicide or find other destructive and counterproductive ways to live their lives.

"'The greatest burden a child must bear is the unlived life of the parents,' **Carl Jung.**

"...there are two reasons to have kids, and only two reasons, ever, one is because you have enough love in your heart and your home, you want to share that with another human being, and that's beautiful, the other is because you failed at whatever you set out to do and you want round two." Steve Hofstetter

No one may give or impose purpose upon their child. Every person must discover their purpose for themselves, by listening to the authentic voice inside that honors their natural talents and capacities and their desire to make a positive impact on the world around them, through their family and friends, their community and their environment. By encouraging your child to recognize that inner truth and by trusting them and trusting yourself, you enable the discovery of purpose in their lives, that will reward them for the rest of their lives.

"The most important thing each of us can know is our unique gift and how to use it in the world. Individuality is cherished and nurtured because, for the whole to flourish, each of us has to be strong in who we are and carry our gifts with conviction, so they can be shared with others."

Braiding Sweetgrass by Robin Wall Zimmerman

Appreciation

Life is a gift. Nothing exists in this world that has not been given to us, by the earth itself and her creator, by our ancestors and parents who bore us, by all those who went before us, inventing and crafting and planting the crops that we harvest and laying the pavement we walk upon and writing the books from we which we learn. Everything is a gift. Appreciation is so important.

Just think of a gift that you have given, something that cost you time or money or effort, the reception that it receives will determine how you feel about your gift and about the recipient. If you cook a meal for someone, and they thank you and enjoy the food, if they notice that you have used the best ingredients or that the harvest came from your own greenhouse, then you will delight in their pleasure, sharing their appreciation and feel that your time and effort and ingredients were well spent.

If you crocheted a blanket or a dress or a pair of socks for your niece and she opened her gift with an expression of distaste or disappointment after you had spent many hours making the gift, thinking of the joy it would bring to someone you loved, not only would you feel hurt and regret the energy that you put into the project for her sake, but you would also feel that she was undeserving of the gift and your efforts. You may very well resolve never to make anything for her again since you know that she will not honor your craft. It is up to you and how you feel about your niece whether you will give her a gift again, but her unappreciation will have tainted your opinion of her, and you shall likely remember the incidents in the future every time it occurs to you to make or buy something for her again. If the gift had gone to a new neighbor or co-worker with whom you had not already established kinship, then it is likely that you would resolve never to give them anything ever again. Appreciation or lack of it makes all the difference in the world.

If you can treat every day as a gift, a blessing that you had not expected to receive (as many people who have experienced a brush with death or a debilitating/degenerating illness discover) then your days will be happy. So often our expectations outweigh our appreciation, thinking about the future and what you feel needs to be accomplished or comparing what you must, expect or hope to have, leaves you living in scarcity, rather than enjoying the fulfillment of all the blessings that you already have. There is nothing like doing without to make you truly appreciate something. Absence makes the heart grow fonder.

Imagine living without electricity or water running from a tap inside of your home for a week or two, a month or two years, then how much more would you appreciate all the time and effort that you are saved once you do have access to these common amenities (that many people take for granted).

Every person wants to feel appreciated, it is an essential component of our sense of worth and identity, to feel that our contribution to the world is essential, valuable. In a society that honors, respects, and appreciates each of its members and resources, all the gifts that have been granted to us by God, Mother Earth, our creator, the Divine. Fulfillment, satisfaction, peace, and harmony would reign over fear, anger, envy, and hate, if we could remember to say, "thank you." What person could envy another if they had all that they truly needed, and were able to appreciate it? What hate or anger could grow if the underlying fears that burdened us were addressed, fear of lack, lack of love, time, basic needs, understanding, value, companionship, resources, and safety?

Want is a very dangerous concept, want has been profoundly exaggerated and projected into the public eye by mass consumerism, advertising and an egocentric society. Want has been sold to us for the sake of profit, yet it profits no one, for want ensares every level of society, the wealthiest billionaires in the world still want more, because enough is never enough. Want is like a cancer, a hunger that feeds and feeds destroying the host without genuinely benefiting anyone. Insatiable hunger is a monster, it is the monster. Every child that cried and cried for comfort, for a mother or father that never came, that hunger that could never have been satisfied by toys, or nannies, or substitutes.

Every evil that corrupted a true need turning it into an insatiable desire, lust, greed, gluttony, envy, pride. To be satisfied with what we have or can reasonably obtain through our own efforts. That is Freedom. Freedom from want.

"In a consumer society, contentment is a radical proposition. Recognizing abundance rather than scarcity undermines an economy that thrives by creating unmet desires. Gratitude cultivates an ethic of fullness."

Braiding Sweetgrass by Robin Wall Zimmerman

How can we instill within our children the capacity and wisdom to recognize satisfaction, to define when enough is enough, to appreciate what they have?

We must all find within ourselves the capacity to appreciate and value what we have and to be satisfied. To recognize when we are happy.

Creativity

Human culture and survival have depended upon the ingenuity of invention, adaptation, modification, and imagination.

"When I was young, in the very last days before television and video games came to dominate American childhood, we created our own worlds with intricate storylines, practicing the ... Technologies that adults can use to fashion their lives and their collective reality; forming a vision, telling a story around that vision that assigns meanings and roles playing

out those roles and so on. Today, those worlds of the imagination come prefabricated from TV studios and software companies, and children wander through cheap, gaudy, often violent worlds created by distant strangers. These come with prefabricated images as well, and the ability to form their own images (we call this ability imagination) atrophies. Unable to envision a new world, the child grows up accustomed to accepting whatever reality is hander her...the technology of the phonograph and radio helped turn music from something people made for themselves into something they paid for. Storage and transportation technologies have done the same for food processing...Are people happier now, more fulfilled, for having films rather than tribal storytellers, mp3 players rather than gathering around the piano? Are we happier eating mass-produced food rather than that from a neighbors' field or our own garden?" **Sacred Economics: Money, Gift, and Society in the Age of Transition by Charles Eisenstein.**

When we try to give too much to our children, we overwhelm them and deny them the capacity to create and discover for themselves.

"only the empty can be filed by Spirit. If you are full, then spirit has no room to enter. Spirit is attracted to the empty spaces within the soul, not to the sites of fullness" **coyote wisdom**

Education

Once you have evaluated the priorities that you have for your child's future and the elements with which you wish them to be educated, it is much easier to define and recognize systems of education that endeavor to cultivate these capacities within your child.

There are many alternatives to consider regarding the education of your child, and it is worth exploring all the options until you find one that you are willing to try. Don't be afraid to make a mistake, or admit that you have if you make one, you can always change if you feel that another method would work better for your child. Children also need to see us make mistakes and recover from them so that they will be able to correct themselves and move on rather than being crushed by failure or stuck in negative patterns.

All children learn differently, and every individual has distinct capacities, strengths, weaknesses, and unique talents. If you recall your own education, you may realize that there is a great deal of material, which you know you covered, which you no longer remember and which you do not use on a daily or even yearly basis. And in spite of this, you have been able to survive competently in the world using the skills and knowledge that you do possess.

It is not necessary to know everything! Thinking about the skills that you do use daily, your ability to read and write, simple arithmetic, practice life skills to specialist work-related capacities, reflection will allow you to realize that you have a great wealth of knowledge and capacity which you can share with your child. Even more than that, you have the ability to find information and learn new things if and when you need to. Thanks to the internet it is even easier than before to access information and if used wisely an internet connection can provide at least as equally full an education as a university degree.

The "constructivist theory" refers to learning by doing and the development of knowledge and understanding based on the child's own interests. It is useful for a child to be exposed to as many different subjects as possible for the child to explore their capacities and to excite their imagination and inspire their passion for learning. **Learning is effortless when our interest and curiosity are stimulated.**

Preserving the passion for learning that every child has, their innate curiosity, is of vital importance. Most people have been structured to consider education as something that terminates with the school bell or with graduation from university. Yet the greatest and most accomplished people in history, those whose skill sets included proficiencies in sciences and humanities, foreign languages, musical instruments and more, are those who knew that you never stop learning. The desire to learn new things can be a passion which inspires and drives someone throughout their entire life. To kill that passion, creates a child who must be forced, reluctant, resistant and unwilling to finish assignments and complete projects, not for their own sense of inner satisfaction and wonderment, but for external influences; threats of punishments or enticements of reward.

The education system used in the public schools, where the underlying assumption is that the minds of the students are empty vessels (empty banks), ready to be filled by other people's ideas and information, without any personal or critical engagement with the concepts, seriously undervalues the individual and can compromise their ability to integrate the information they are trying to learn.

Many alternative systems of education recognize that by following the innate skills, needs and interests of the child, that is, by listening to the child and their needs, it is easier to educate them and provide them with information in such a way as to preserve and augment their natural curiosity and love of learning.

The world is fascinating, everything is interesting. If you have ever had an inspiring teacher, you will know that they were able to make you interested in their topic of expertise whatever it was. Inspirational teachers share information in such a way that you felt that learning is a pleasurable experience, even if you had not previously enjoyed that subject.

Conversely, a bad teacher (and I am sure that most people will have encountered someone like this) can make you hate a subject that you previously loved, and even dissuade you from pursuing that subject in the future. A bad teacher can effectively kill the love and joy of learning that you feel for that subject. It is so important to have teachers that truly love and feel enthusiastic about the subject that they are teaching, however, in the modern education system many teachers feel constricted by scheduled curriculum and stressed over test score and performance ratings that their own love and enjoyment of teaching can be affected.

Within the standard school system, most parents will be aware that there is a great deal of difference regarding test results, college applications and academic or sporting success depending on the school. Many parents seek out private schools and move to school districts which have excellent reputations in the hopes of securing the best education possible for their child. Private schools and academies often offer specialties, from schools strong in the visual arts, sports, and music to those specializing in languages such as bilingual schools, or religious schools, military academies, and theater schools. Most of the schools offer the general government standardized school curriculum supplemented by teachers, trainers, and coaches with acknowledged expertise in the desired area of specialty.

There are also other schools which offer alternative systems of education. Rather than follow the government prescribed school curriculum, many of these schools offer their own curriculum and provide standard government tests at the end of each year or at graduation, to measure the capacities of the children against their contemporaries in the typical school system.

I will endeavor to introduce some of the most popular and well known alternative systems of education below and the philosophies which inspire them. I encourage you to do your own investigations and research to find a pedagogical philosophy that speaks to you and your partner. Once you have made your decision, remember to observe your child, their enjoyment of learning, their school environment and comprehension and their progress to make sure that the system of education works equally well for them.

Montessori Schools

Maria Montessori was the first female doctor ever qualified in Italy. She spent time during her early career working in the pediatric department of an asylum. Children diagnosed with mental illnesses at that time, including those with down syndrome, autism, and other learning difficulties were often sent off to asylums where they were clothed and fed and kept clean, but offered no stimulation, education or human interaction. They experienced a very poor quality of life, having been abandoned by their families and society in general.

Maria Montessori began to implement changes within the institution where she worked, bringing in materials that she designed herself at her own expense to attempt to teach the children and offer them a better quality of life. After working with her specially developed didactic materials, Montessori was able to determine that the children in her care demonstrated an extraordinary development. They had even been brought up to the same standard of education as their peers in public school, reading, writing and completing basic arithmetic as well as taking care of themselves and their environment. Her results were astounding and implemented a great deal of change in the treatment of the previously neglected children by state and private institutions. Maria Montessori believed that if her techniques could provide such excellent results in children with learning difficulties, then they would surely have an even more profound effect on children with typical capacities.

At the time, the government was organizing the first publicly funded housing initiative for the poorest members of society. However, there was a great deal of vandalism by the children, who were often left unsupervised and uneducated by their parents during the day as many of them worked at night, walking the streets and committing thefts and other crimes. The parents themselves did not know how to care for the properties either, never having been taught or provided with the opportunity to live in homes of their own.

Since repairing from vandalism was such a great expense, Maria Montessori took the opportunity to propose that one apartment in one of the buildings be turned into a school where she volunteered her time and raised funds from philanthropic women of society to attempt to implement her new-found methods of teaching with all the children of the block. One of the greatest gifts, she said, was the lack of adequate funding to hire a professional teacher. Instead, she hired maids as assistants and was able to implement her new method of education without any resistance from those schooled in the formal system of education.

Maria Montessori believed that listening to the child, and observing their needs, interactions and stages of development were key to designing a system of education. One that could impart information to the children at the exact time that they were most capable and interested in learning it, and through a means that satisfied the child's natural development. Her first school was an astounding success, turning poor, neglected children into apt and intelligent students who took pride and care in their own appearance, the care of their school and the educational materials. Through this method, children as young as four years old were able to read and write, without ever feeling that they had been forced.

Maria Montessori's method of education relies heavily on didactic materials, specially designed (and continuously adapted by Maria Montessori until she was fully satisfied) to teach children about different aspects of their environment.

Each apparatus is designed to simplify concepts, encapsulating one single investigative and experiential aspect each and make it self-correcting so that the child can study on their own with the material and work out when they are getting it right.

Concentration is very important to a child and Maria Montessori observed that children left on their own to play often dedicated themselves to repeating the same action repeatedly (when uninterrupted) and in this way (almost scientifically) they built up their knowledge of the act and their understanding of the world and its natural laws. Montessori also noticed that children were rarely provided with the opportunity to carry out their experiments to their fruition or to their own satisfaction. Often the children were interrupted by (well-meaning) parents and teachers who did not understand the nature of what the child was doing and tried to "help" by doing it for them or by removing the object from their child lest it be broken.

As Montessori observed breaking the child's developing concentration and its own natural repetitive contemplations and investigations has a very detrimental effect on a child, interrupting their natural development and capacity to learn. Maria Montessori considered children who had been interrupted too often unable to concentrate consequently. When "rehabilitating" students from the standard system of education a period of adjustment was necessary before the Montessori system could be applied and the didactic materials introduced.

All children attending a Montessori school are carefully observed and provided ample opportunity to develop this level of concentration. Once this extended period of focus and the continuous repetition of a task is observed a child returns to its natural path of inner learning, this child (within the Montessori system) is said to be normalized.

Maria Montessori noted that it is impossible for anyone to teach anything to a child. A child must learn themselves through observation, imitation, and experimentation. The best that an educator can hope to do is to provide the best possible environment and materials for the child to develop and provide them with the uninterrupted opportunity to conduct their experiments by themselves.

Once a child has become normalized (that is they have demonstrated they have returned to their innate pattern of concentration and investigation) they are introduced to didactic materials one at a time by a teacher who (without talking) demonstrates the precise use of the didactic material and then invites the child to attempt to repeat the exercise. All the materials are set up progressively in a specific order, and no child can use materials until they have been introduced to them. However, they are able to use any of the materials that they have previously learned how to use, and often teach younger children.

Children are discouraged from using the materials in any way other than its designed use (measuring rods, for example, are not allowed to be employed as a flying airplane) and if misappropriated the material is taken away until the child is ready to concentration on it again.

Some criticism of the Montessori method suggests that this limits imaginative play. *"the child learns by imitating, and his most important activity is play. The modern tendency to force intellectual learning on young children, and to structure their lives with classes, lessons and team sports, deprives children of the vital development that accrues from unstructured, imaginative play, and can have serious consequences on the child's emotional and intellectual development.* **"The Nourishing Traditions Book of Baby & Child Care Morell, Sally Fallon; Morell, Sally Fallon; Cowan, Thomas S.; Cowan, Thomas S**

In the Montessori method of education, children are encouraged to play as they wish during recess, just not with didactic materials. Usually, classrooms are set up so that there is an inside and outside environment (such as a little garden) that is accessible to the children always. The design of the classroom is fundamental, and the environment must be kept beautiful (and not too cluttered). Children are encouraged to keep order, to respect each other and to become involved in the care of their environment by taking on chores such as laying the table, sweeping the floor, gardening, etc.

Practical life skills are a very valuable part of this education system. Only one set of each didactic material is provided, and children are encouraged to wait their turn if someone else is already using what they wish to use. Each activity must be put away carefully before a new activity can be started. A great deal of responsibility is intentionally cultivated in this system, as well as instilling within children attention to detail and presentation.

Children are educated in mixed age groups, originally from 2 ½ years of age up until 6. However, most modern classes break this down into groups of no more than 3 years difference. Social education of children through mixed age groups allows younger children to follow the positive example of the older children, imitating their behavior and provides the opportunity for the older children to teach the younger, reinforcing their own understanding of the material and how to communicate with others. Students will stay with one class teacher for each of the three-year periods and go on to join fellow that they knew from previous years as they advance to the next class.

Preschool and Primary Montessori schools are more popular and easy to find. However, some Montessori schools do provide education all the way through secondary education, and experiential learning and hands-on application of knowledge is a significant aspect of the curriculum, with practical life skills and responsibilities continuing to be highlighted throughout the education.

The Montessori method is very rewarding when correctly applied (although there are unfortunate cases of schools claiming to use the Montessori method which provide the didactic materials but fail to observe the correct protocol of introducing the materials to the students, which undermines the results of the method and the child's education).

Although some Montessori schools in European countries are subsidized by the government, most Montessori schools in other parts of the world are private and require payment. All teachers trained in the Montessori method must have completed a bachelor's degree before starting the

Montessori teacher training and are often quite well paid in comparison to teachers in the public sector.

It is worthwhile investigating this method of education. A great deal of information is available for educating children within the home from birth to age 3, before many of the other alternative systems of education begin.

Waldorf-Steiner Schools

Austrian philosopher Rudolf Steiner founded the first Waldorf School in Germany in 1919, based on his philosophy called Anthroposophy (Greek for human wisdom). There are now over 1,000 Waldorf schools in 38 countries, and Waldorf education is among the largest and fastest-growing independent education movements in the world. Rudolph Steiner wrote and lectured extensively regarding a vast range of subjects including farming (Biodynamics), art, dance (Eurythmics), diet, architecture, biology, history, geology, finance, medicine, and education. Anthroposophy is concerned with the spiritual evolution of the individual and society and incorporates astrology, astronomy, meditation, Christian mysticism, Karma, reincarnation, and clairvoyance, amongst other disciplines. Steiner schools follow a curriculum based on the observations of Rudolph Steiner concerning the developmental stages of childhood and claim to take a holistic approach to educating the child.

*"Steiner believed that within every human being was an "ideal human being," a complete and harmonious ego capable of giving love in perfect freedom; and that only such human beings could give rise to a harmonious, just and free human community. "**The Nourishing Traditions Book of**

Within the Waldorf/Steiner system, formal education does not begin until 7, because the first seven years of a child's life are dedicated to the exploration of the world through play, imagination, rhythm, stories and the arts. The next phase of development in the child is marked by their losing their milk teeth and developing their adult teeth, this is on average around age 7, and it is at this stage that children are taught to read and write. The Steiner system considers it detrimental to the natural development of the child to teach children to read before this age. Another developmental stage occurs around age 14 and is marked by puberty, and at age 21 the individual is a fully manifest individual.

Steiner school education encourages children to play with toys made from natural materials and to use their imagination wherever possible (for this reason Steiner dolls and puppets do not include any details on the face). Parents are encouraged not to expose their children to television, video games and other artificially produced stimulation which is considered an impediment to the child's own creativity, overwhelming them through over-stimulation, and potentially corrupting and endangering the innocence of childhood.

As well as their emphasis on the arts, which encourages hands-on creative exploration through all subjects, the Steiner method also emphasizes the need for children to learn experientially, by doing, therefore, many activities such as gardening and circus skills, will often be found on the timetable as well as Eurythmics dance and other physical activities which encourage hand-eye coordination, motor skills, and balance. The Waldorf/Steiner method also produces strong results in the sciences and mathematics. All children are taught two foreign languages from their first schooling year (age 7) and receive three years of oral tuition in each foreign language before introducing the grammar. Children are usually educated in groups defined by age; however, they stay with one form teacher for several years. The idea is that this provides stability for the children and a greater understanding of the development and learning needs of the individual student. My own experience of teachers has proven to me that although this is a wonderful opportunity when an individual student has a positive rapport with their teacher if a child has a bad relationship with their teacher, then it is a shame to be stuck with them over an extended period.

While the curriculum of Steiner schools is based upon the original Anthroposophical influences of Rudolph Steiner, Steiner schools in recent years have been keen to distance their education system from Anthroposophy and explain that they neither teach nor promote the broader philosophy known as Anthroposophy to their students. Steiner schools do not follow the standardized government curriculum. Instead students take a national exam at age 14, when they are expected to be on the same academic level as students in the typical school system (remember that students start formal education 2 years later than average and that the Waldorf education claims to offer additional subjects and many other advantages to the children they teach).

Within the curriculum, rather than teach the students several subjects continuously, subjects such as math are studied in depth in blocks over a period of three to five weeks. Once the subject has been explored thoroughly, the class moves on to another subject such as geography, returning to math in the next year, when they are able to tackle a more advanced level. The complete Waldorf curriculum has been likened to an ascending spiral: subjects are revisited several times, but each new exposure affords greater depth and new insights into the topic.

There is also a great deal of crossover between subjects, with the intention of integrating knowledge in practical work such as gardening which incorporates biology, art, math (how many seeds, how much space, so forth), geography, weather cycles, etc. There are also many other practical courses such as carpentry, pattern making (which use geometry and measurements), as well as artistic exploration in science, such as collages of photosynthesis and life cycles. Art is believed to elicit an emotional connection to academic work that deepens awareness, understanding, appreciation, and retention of the material being studied.

The Waldorf/Steiner system of education is appropriate for all children. The system has had a particularly high-level of success with children experiencing learning difficulties such as dyslexia, ADHD, Downs Syndrome and Autism. Children with learning difficulties are often educated in the same class as their peers, although the teacher has input regarding new additions and how they may affect the balance of the class as a whole. There are also some specialty schools and communities throughout the world designed to teach children with specific learning challenges. Many schools often adopt alternative medicine, such as homeopathy in treating children and encourage positive nature-based nutrition.

Some Steiner schools can be found publicly funded in the United Kingdom and Scandinavia. However, they are rare, and most Steiner schools are prohibitively expensive for more impoverished families. Many schools do offer limited bursary and scholarship places, so if you are interested, do investigate the schools within your local area.

The Steiner system of education has been specifically developed to encourage the natural curiosity, creativity, and love of learning in children, they also publicize their promotion of self-motivation, problem-solving and critical thinking, encouraging children to experiment and think for themselves rather than memorize the results of others. There is tremendous emphasis on preserving the innocence of childhood and protecting children from the fast-paced influences of the greater society that has, through advertising and media began to encroach upon childhood.

The latest example of this is the relatively new term and concept of "tween" which has been developed to create a new market within a consumerist society. Thus, encouraging children to grow up quickly, imitating adult behavior, clothing, accessories and obsession with labels, rather than honoring and preserving the freedom of childhood from such vanities and concerns. The increased pressure on younger children to imitate the buying habits and lifestyle of celebrities has led to even younger children to acquire lifelong addictions, eating disorders and developmental crises.

Steiner education seems to embrace the view that children were once content to play with sticks, mud, leaves and anything else they could find in the garden, not merely because their parents could not afford to purchase anything better, but because the children had something much more valuable (and worth cultivating) imagination. The child's own creativity filled in the blanks and turned that stick into a walking stick, a pirate's sword, an arrow for a bow, a flag pole, a drum stick, etc. etc. etc.

Helsinki Schools

The Finnish system of education is one of the highest-ranking education systems in the world. For nine consecutive years, they were at the top of the PISA results comparing international education, and have continued to rank very highly, along with several Asian countries such as Hong Kong, Shanghai, and Korea. PISA results have consistently ranked education in the United States and the United Kingdom as below average.

The Finnish system of education does things a little differently. Unlike some Oriental models of education which put a lot of pressure on children to perform academically, work hard, spend long hours in school and take home large amounts of homework (even from a young age), the Finnish system of education has managed to get incredible results by taking a softer approach.

Within the Finnish system of education, children do not start school and formal education until age 7 (although there is preschool from age 6). Children study no more than 5 hours per day, often starting school at 9 am, and they take home very little homework, less than 3 hours per week, all the way up into secondary school. Children are provided a 15-minute break after each 1-hour lesson, in which they are encouraged to play outside, in all weather conditions (appropriate clothing applied). Half of Finland is in the Arctic Circle, so it is cold there, yet they recognize that access to fresh air and the natural environment encourages good health and helps the body to adapt to extreme changes in temperature. Class sizes are usually small, a maximum of 20 students per class, and school sizes are also diminutive.

Rather than putting pressure on children to perform, through a paradigm of punishment and reward, children are encouraged, through their culture, society, home life and school, to view their education as their own responsibility, and a blessing for which they should be grateful. Teachers are well respected in the Finnish culture, with very high standards. Every teacher must have completed a masters level in their chosen field of education or in pedagogy, and the profession is well paid. Schools are encouraged to develop their own curriculum, which means that teachers feel free to adapt their coursework and lesson plans to meet the needs and interests of their students, rather than being micro-managed.

Students are required to sit through evaluations such as pop quizzes and test throughout their education. However, there is only one formal standard examination which occurs during their last year of school. There is also a choice within the upper levels of schools where children can dedicate themselves to academic studies or vocational studies. These are both equally regarded by society, and vocational studies are more likely to feed into a profession directly after school, whereas, academic studies are more likely to lead to higher education. There is, however, flexibility, and children have a chance to change their mind or to repeat their course. In the upper years, the students are also able to structure their own timetable, with courses usually taking 3 years. Individuals can choose a more intensive course of study which can be completed within 2 years or choose a less demanding structure which takes 4 years to complete.

This means that the brightest children can complete their studies quicker and move on to higher levels of education rather than getting bored or wasting their time. Other students with additional obligations such as a part-time job, a child or family member to care for or extracurricular activities that take up a great deal of their time, are able to adapt their studies to meet their obligations rather than risk sacrificing their education altogether.

While not everyone can choose to move to Finland, there are several initiatives to bring the Finnish model of education to other parts of the world, including Helsinki schools. As with all the methods of education mentioned here, I encourage you to do your own research and explore your options if this style of education appeals to you.

Free Schools, Democratic Schools & De-Schooling

Imagine a world where all doors are open, a world without age segregation, a safe world, where children were welcomed everywhere. Where a child could walk into a lawyer's office, a science lab, a hospital, backstage at an opera company, into a mechanics workshop or into the kitchen of their favorite restaurant. Within these children would find professionals, and experts, performing any number of real-life tasks and could learn from these masters in their field, how to perform these practical tasks and the theory and reason behind them. Imagine, rather than being frustrated by interruption, every person was predisposed to take pleasuring in satisfying the curiosity of a child and was happy to dedicate their time and knowledge to teaching that child as much as they were interested in knowing, even letting the child try for themselves, how to dice garlic, or tighten the nuts and bolts within an engine, disinfect a wound or apply a bandage.

It reminds me of the way that young children learn, asking questions, watching, trying for themselves. Children are naturally curious and will ask anything and everything whenever they discover something that interests them. That interest, that desire for understanding and knowledge and capacity is what drives the independent learner to study. It is a motivation that comes from within, an inspiration to tackle subjects and exercises that we do not necessarily enjoy, because we understand that the outcome of following the grammar of a language or the laws of physics will help us to speak and create and invent fluently, expressing our creativity in the world.

The world, of course, is not like this. Even though some children are fortunate enough to have a relationship with their family where they can ask questions and learn how to accomplish the many chores and tasks that they see performed around their home, all aspects of society are not open to the public and certainly not to school-aged children.

The entire universe does not revolve around each child, and many actions cannot be interrupted, halted, postponed or performed in front of others. A chef in a restaurant cannot stop to teach a child when they have customers waiting, and a doctor cannot always perform an operation in front of a young student.

However, within the concept of the free school movement, the idea is that workshops and classes are being conducted by teachers and experts in their fields and children are able to choose (just as they may be given the right to choose extracurricular activities) whether they wish to attend or not, depending upon their knowledge and interests at the time.

The idea is the child, no matter what their age, is respected as an autonomous individual, fully capable of making all decisions that relate to their own education, and that they are not obligated by any external pressure to study subjects that they do not have an interest in.

Within many free schools, children can choose for themselves whether they wish to play or study, and what they wish to study depending upon what classes and teachers are available at the time. Timetables exist only for the teachers.

Adopting a democratic system of self-government, rules of conduct, consequences from breaking the rules, damaging property, etc. are all made by the students and teachers together in grand assemblies and meetings where every member has an equal vote and an equal say.

Not only do children get to choreograph the schedule of lessons and workshops available to them, they even get to vote on which teachers and staff are hired and rehired each year. Imagine having the power to choose only those teachers that really inspire you. Imagine teachers being motivated to teach their students in such a way that those children would prefer to be in their class rather than doing anything else, rather than being forced to adhere to guidelines set by government bodies that never attend or benefit from their classes.

For many children, their own uninterrupted interest in learning new things motivates them to make commitments to specific classes and workshops on a regular basis. However, schools often report that children transferring into free school environments from mainstream schooling take a while to adjust, often choosing to play all day, and not attend lessons for weeks or months at a time.

"Interest is the only criterion for engaging in any activity, and satisfaction the only evaluation of success...When a student has a serious interest, there is no stopping her, and "making it fun" is often an intolerable distraction. When a student has an interest, we believe she should be allowed to pursue it only as far as she feels necessary. She may return to an important idea later, to deepen her interest, but forcing or manipulating her to deepen it will only serve to lessen her curiosity and sense of self-determination." **What is (and isn't) a democratic school? By Den Demokratiske Skole**

Children know what makes them happy. All too often schools and institutions contradict that innate capacity in the child and train them to forget how much they enjoy learning; democratic schools endeavor to empower the child's inner compass providing them with the opportunity to obtain practical skills for their lives while preserving their autonomy and self-motivation. The academic results of these schools are not considered to be an accurate reflection of their contribution since results are often less than competitive. Nor is it the main focus or priority of this system of schooling. Every individual is provided with the opportunity to discover their vocation in life, that is the profession or course of action that provides them with the most amount of happiness, whether that leads to a career as a fashion designer, street sweeper or university professor. The idea of this education is to honor the inherent worth of the individual and respect their right to choose what is best for themselves rather than a parent or teacher forcing their idea and concept of what is right upon the child. Cooperation and responsibility are encouraged through the mutual relationship of the society which exists within the school and the rules that they choose to enforce within themselves. The child is also spared the time and effort of studying subjects which they do not enjoy, which do not interest them, and which do not relate to the profession that they choose to pursue in the future. I know there is much of my own education I do not recall or employ within my daily life and which I do not feel has contributed in any particularly positive way to my life (such as battle dates from history class, however for a historian, a history teacher, an archaeologist or a museum cataloger these facts may be essential and even fascinating).

Long ago most people were educated through on-the-job-apprenticeships, with children learning their work from their parents, helping with daily chores around the house, the farm, and the workshop. Parents of children who wished to learn another trade had to pay for an apprenticeship position since the master was often responsible for room and board as well as an expert education. Many children missed out on learning what they wished, there was sadly a lot of mistreatment from abusive masters. Once the industrial revolution took place and many crafts and professions were taken over by machinery and factories, society developed industrial systems of education to prepare students to fulfill new roles in the workplace, as well as to provide universal childcare for the new factory workers.

Apprenticeships worked very well for centuries, and recognition of this has begun to make a comeback in the form of vocational studies. All work as an apprentice would have been experiential and produced the many craftsmen and experts needed at all levels of society at the time. On the job training.

Our neurology is stimulated by sensory input, we are designed to learn experientially, it is our optimal method of learning, by doing, by being, by absorbing multi-sensory learning, interactive learning, that activates our minds and our bodies on a physiological, neurological and biochemical level.

Many students and employers are increasingly dissatisfied with the level of education provided by the regular school system and universities which turn out hundreds of thousands of students with fresh qualifications every year. A university degree is no longer enough to make someone stand out from the crowd, and many firms require that newly qualified employees enter internships (often unpaid) and attend other in-house education and training programs to prepare them to meet the needs of their employers.

When you consider the vast financial expenses and the number of years of a young person's life dedicated to acquiring university qualifications, (many students ending up deep in debt), it is not surprising that the current conveyor belt of education has received a great deal of criticism. Ivan Illich wrote of the hypocrisy of the indoctrinating systems of education which produce institutionalized students with standardized education, where the products (qualified graduates) are indistinguishable from one another. In his critique Deschooling Society. *"Schools,"* he said, *"teach the need to be taught."*

Ivan Illich is critical of authoritarian systems of education in which *"some men may set, specify, and evaluate the personal goals of others."* He also makes comparisons with contemporary unschooled societies in which children are not segregated and removed from society because of their age being "boxed away in schools" but instead integrate into every level of their community, learning their roles and obligations through example and practice.

Illich claimed that:

1. Most learning happens informally.
2. Institutionalized schooling hinders true learning.
3. The ideal education "system" allows people to choose what they learn and when they learn.

The majority of democratic and free schools are private, and therefore, attract fee-paying pupils and parents, meaning many pupils have come from wealthy families. Although most of the children who have passed through these systems of education feel blessed by the opportunity, and indeed have progressed to find employment in a wide range of careers, some former students have expressed regret at the difficulty they found adjusting to university and the work environment where they recognized great gaps of information in their learning (which they were obligated to catch up on in their own time). They were also less inclined to feel pressured by hierarchical systems of authority within their place of employment. Whether you consider this to be a good thing or not will depend upon your ideology, however, nonconformity is not always well appreciated by employers. Many former pupils have gone on to create their own businesses where they are the boss or have been provided with the opportunity to take a place within a family business, where their eccentricities could be accepted or compensated for.

As with all the alternative school systems mentioned, and even the normal school system, this educational ideology can work wonders for some students, and is best under ideal circumstances. However, it important to follow your child and their enthusiasm and progress through their education to evaluate whether it is truly appropriate in their individual case.

Jamie, creator of The Self-Made Scholar website, provides thought provoking comments on the programmed mentality of children who have received most of their education from the mainstream schooling system and suggests that during the transition period of recovery from institutionalized education, there are often two major challenges which need to be overcome, these are the f/mentality, and the a/mentality.

Those students who have failed classes and consistently experiences poor academic results in their schooling (say rather that the education system failed them), have often internalized this external projection of their worth and capacity, their biggest challenge is in believing in their own capacity to learn and in discovering their passion for learning, which often demands great psychological strength, when they have been consistently taught that they are weak and to doubt themselves. Self-doubt is not humility, it is not a virtue, but a debilitating mental limitation, which serves no positive purpose except to suppress and subjugate individuals.

Interestingly enough, the second challenge is faced by the a/students, those who have consistently performed to the expectations of their teachers and the standard system of education. These students have become accustomed to being evaluated externally, and manipulating their own opinions and productivity that they have effectively been trained to submit and serve not their own creativity or their own ideals but authority. Like Pavlov's dogs, they are trained to respond to the bell.

"Attending class was a high – teachers complimented me, my papers were passed around as examples, I almost always got A's. The more A's I got, the more I wanted to get. ...If you think an A means "learned well," think again. In almost all classes, an A means "did what the teacher wanted him/her to do." All you must do to get good grades in college is to pick up on the personality nuances of the teacher and turn in work accordingly. If you want A's, don't write your ideas in an essay, write what the teacher wants you to write. Play the system. Answer questions from the teacher's perspective...

The "play the system" thinking that "A-students" develop is good for grades, but bad for the brain. It kills the natural desire to learn and replaces it with a cheap sense of accomplishment."

"It rings a bell and the young man in the middle of writing a poem must close his notebook and move to different cell where he must memorize that man and monkeys derive from a common ancestor."

http://selfmadescholar.com/b/2009/03/31/great-thinkers-on-self-education-john-taylor-gatto/

The result of their education is that the "A-student" will continue to pursue external praise from perceived authority figures, the boss, society, peer pressure, advertising etc. Their "A-grade" of success is just as likely to stand for the education system's success in indoctrinating the individual to conform, as it is in commending academic capability.

Spiritual empowerment never comes from giving away responsibility, control and power to authority, every individual is responsible for their own actions, their own morals, and their own soul. Where an individual is able to govern and discipline themselves and hold themselves up to their own high standards and codes of honor, then they will know true freedom and the responsibility which comes with that freedom. The responsibility of freedom is heavy, and it requires maturity, just as a child must learn to take responsibility for caring for their own basic needs in order to become an independent adult, the individual must take responsibility for their own conduct in all things, to achieve spiritual maturity.

When this happens, you may find people making mistakes, but you will not hear the excuse "because they made me do it" or see the kinds of horrors and atrocities performed on a grand scale by people following orders, such as was found in Nazi concentration camps, and has been seen repeated continuously throughout the world, in war torn countries, through ethnic genocides, invasions, and economic exploitations.

Every choice must be accounted for and taking responsibility for one's own life and one's own actions can be as simple as choosing to buy fair trade and organic or to dedicate one's life to the care of orphans. Choosing to turn a blind eye, and to ignore the reality of suffering and injustice, is also a choice. All religions and spiritual philosophies agree that every person is ultimately responsible for themselves, their actions, choices, and consequences. Although it seems sometimes that consequences can be perpetually deferred, eventually we will reap what we sow, the deteriorating state of the global environment and its diminishing clean resources is just one testament to that.

Home Education

There are many reasons to opt out of public school, from competition, to the preservation of innocence, to protecting your child from influences that you cannot control. Every child will be educated and influenced morally and otherwise by their peers. Many children spend more time, hour for hour with the other children in their class than they do with their working parents, so unless all the children in your school share common ideologies, from a religious or Theosophical point of view like church schools and Waldorf schools support then you are unlikely to be able to determine what influences your children are exposed to.

From seemingly innocent influences such as the introduction of make-up, nail varnish and short skirts to preteens, consumerism which influences children to prioritize designer labels, and video games, to swearing, violence, drug use, pornography, and drinking, etc. so many influences on your children will come from the peers they associate with and the material that they are exposed to via the media (T.V., music, video games).

As a parent, it is 100% your responsibility to care for your child, their upbringing and their education, even if you do not educate your child yourself, you are responsible for choosing who you entrust the care and education of your child. There are no excuses, and you do not want to turn around one day and find that your child is someone that you do not know, do not recognize and do not understand.

Unlike the previous alternative systems of education, there is no one unifying theory or philosophy which dictates the various methods used by parents to educate their children at home, except perhaps for their belief in their own capacity to do so. Many parents find themselves home educating their children by accident after having discovered that their child was doing poorly in traditional schools. Sometimes exceptionally bright children, those "twice gifted" (with a learning difficulty such as dyslexia, coupled with above average intelligence), those with learning difficulties, and other special needs such as ADHD children find that traditional schools do not offer the best education and environment and their parents choose to take matters into their own hands by educating at home.

Within standardized systems of education more and more children are being encouraged to take medication such as Ritalin to adapt to the need of the school, rather than the school and educational system adapting to the needs of the child. Many hyperactive and ADHD children have high levels of energy and find it difficult to sit still for long periods of time and focus on one subject, often their curiosity and quick paced learning means that their mind flies from one subject to another. These children need to be stimulated and their interest engaged, rather than being drugged so that they can sit still during class.

Many adults would envy the level of energy that these children demonstrate, and such energy can often be positively channeled into a dance or sport, which has multiple beneficial effects for the child (but which often require additional funding, pills are cheaper). I do not consider it to be a surprise that more and more children are being diagnosed with these conditions at the same time that children are (often for the sake of safety from strangers- the most dangerous predators our offspring face) being confined to smaller and smaller places, within cities and blocks of flats where they are fed television and video games to entertain their minds and distract them from the inactivity of their bodies rather than being free to run in and out of their back gardens or the farmyard at leisure.

I was not sure whether to marvel at the ingenuity or despair at the sad state of current social trends when I discovered that some schools have begun to introduce desks with built-in bicycles for students to burn off excess energy while studying in the classroom. (Perhaps connected to the electrical grid these children could provide the renewable energy to supply their schools lights and heating etc. From slave powered empires to oil powered global economies and back again. The Workhouse.)

There are many reasons to choose to home educate your child. Many people choose to home educate their child for religious or cultural reasons, choosing to educate their children in a way that is adapted to their own beliefs and ideals. Others, as I mentioned, choose to home educate their children as a solution to problems that they found with the mainstream education system, including bullying. Some children are home educated for short periods of time, during an illness or when families are required to move to foreign countries temporarily for work. For others however, it is a lifestyle choice. In fact, home-schooling does not require a home at all, road-schooling is a relatively popular concept of home educating one's children while traveling the world, often in a motor-home, caravan, or boat.

Many parents believe that exposing their children to alternative cultures, languages, foods, religions, environments, animals, climates etc. during travel contributes to their education, adding a practical, experiential level to subjects such as geography, religious studies, anthropology, biology, languages and many more areas of interest. By exposing their children to vastly different cultures they are also ensuring that their child sees there are many different options when it comes to life, and future employment.

The child is constantly exposed to new interests and activities that excite their minds and inspire their interest and curiosity. Visits to museums and art galleries can take place throughout the world and even a simple visit to shops can involve speaking a foreign language and calculating currency exchange rates. Some interests are also transferable and sports such as bike riding, swimming, running, yoga and others can be practiced by children and their families almost anywhere.

There are also a great many ways to approach the curriculum that is offered to children. Many parents simply choose to follow their country's recommended curriculum, purchasing school supplies, textbooks and lesson plans from companies which specialize in these products (there are an overwhelming number of these available), which are known as "boxed curriculum." Often, parents choose (or are required by their state or countries government) to arrange for their child to sit for standardized tests each year in order to measure their progress and compare it to their contemporaries in mainstream education.

Some schools will offer the option of acting as a cover school to help guide parents in educating their children and arranging for tests to be conducted in supervised environments. Another option now available includes online cyber schools. It is very important to investigate the laws within your own country, to discover what flexibility, you have as a parent regarding the education of your child as rules and regulations vary widely, even from state to state in the USA. In some circumstances, limited funding may be available.

Some parents choose to educate their children using tutors, something like the hiring of a governess for the education of the children of the house in days gone by. This of course can be costly, however, some parents compromise by hiring private tutors for some subjects such as music lessons and sending their children to group activities such as gymnastics, while taking care of the reading, writing, and arithmetic at home, with the aid of age-appropriate textbooks and workbooks.

Other parents choose to set their own curriculum. Unschooling is a philosophy of education which very closely mirrors the ideals of the free school/democratic schools. Parents follow their children's lead to determine what subject to study and for how long, such as an interest in sharks becoming the inspirations for library visits, museum visits, documentaries and even cooking experiments with shark fin soup.

"I've noticed a fascinating phenomenon in my 25 years of teaching — that schools and schooling are increasingly irrelevant to the great enterprises of the planet. No one believes anymore that scientists are trained in science classes or politicians in civics classes or poets in English classes. The truth is that schools don't really teach anything except how to obey orders. This is a great mystery to me because thousands of humane, caring people work in schools as teachers and aides and administrators, but the abstract logic of the institution overwhelms their individual contributions. Although teachers do care and do work very hard the institution is psychopathic, it has no conscience." **John Taylor Gatto**

Most parents settle on an eclectic mix which suits their own timetable, abilities, resources, and funding, as well as fits in with their educational ideologies. The options are endless; however, it is important to remember there are a wide variety of regulations to ensure that children are not neglected and often the bureaucracy of dealing with paperwork and record taking for government bodies requires a great deal of dedication and time on the part of the parents.

It is often helpful to seek out support groups either of other parents home educating in your area or within your specialty, such as catering to children with specific learning difficulties or based upon the Montessori principles. Support groups can often help those who are just getting started by providing experience on how to deal with issues such as paperwork, school schedules, timetabling, social interaction etc.

With home education, your child requires a great deal of self-discipline and responsibility and the outcome will depend entirely on the amount of effort that you put in and the methods that you choose, as well as the cooperation of your children.

Some parents find it overwhelming to homeschool their children, unless they use private tutors. It can require the same level of dedication and investment as a full-time career, and since stay at home parents or those working from home do not get the relief of changing their environment by coming home after work, many parents often experience stress, and burnout, running out of enthusiasm or creating a stressful learning environment for and relationship between themselves and their child. This is one reason why a support group of other home educating parents and other activities that provide an opportunity for the parents (and children) to refresh their batteries is vital to the healthy relationship of your family.

A possible alternative is to set up a community or co-operative school with other like-minded parents and teachers which provide the opportunity for parents to have control of their child curriculum, without requiring that they undertake responsibility for every aspect of their child's care and education by themselves. A parent can choose to use whichever skills they feel most confident in and enjoy performing, such as choosing to cook healthy nutritious school meals for all the children, or offering to teach carpentry etc. By sharing their skills, the children benefit from the wealth of knowledge of all the members of the co-operative community and since the attitude of the teachers is so vital, choosing to teach what you enjoy will be of even greater benefit to the children as your positive attitude will inspire their own love of the subject and make the experience fun and enjoyable even if it is not their own first choice.

One of the most important things to remember is that as a home-schooling parent you are also learning, and you must endeavor to forgive your own mistakes and set positive examples for your children by continuing your own self-study and research to investigate pedagogy. Learning is effortless when something inspires your curiosity, teaching is effortless when you enjoy the topic and you want to share the information and the passion that you feel for it.

Seek the effortless path, teaching should be fun, your relationship with your children should be firm, guiding, but harmonious, keep trying new things until you get there, and if all else fails to return to the wisdom that birth teaches us, surrender, listen to instinct and follow your child's lead.

Co-operative Schools

There are a variety of different types of co-operative schools, from groups of parents who have banded together to share the responsibility of educating their children (something like home education only expanded to small communities of like-minded parents, who share the responsibility of teaching different subjects), to large government sponsored academies. Each different type of co-operative is designed upon a different co-operative model, you can have teacher co-operatives, parent-co-operatives, and trust run co-operatives. Each model is very different and reflects the needs of different aspects of the school society. However, co-operative schools do not necessarily deviate from the standard curriculum, although they can accommodate any type of pedagogy, they are instead different approaches to organizing the administrative running of the schools.

Teacher run co-operatives, for example, often provide more support, higher pay, additional health benefits and pension options for teachers, who administer the schools funding for the mutual benefit of all the school's employees. Parent run co-operatives on the other hand allow parents to have more input in the running of their children's schools. Parents hire teachers as employees and often provide additional support as teaching assistants, school bus drivers, dinner ladies and administration staff. Parents are responsible for hiring and firing teachers, modifying the curriculum and class schedule and may even have a say on what kinds of meals are served to their children. Trust run co-operatives are organized by non-profit trusts which employ all the school employees from teaching staff, to the school governing body. As with all co-operatives, these systems are based upon democracy, with each member carrying an equal vote.

Many parents who are interested in the co-operative method are also often more open minded when it comes to considering alternative method of education, so it is worth investigating every co-operative school individually, as they will vary greatly in how they educate children. If there is nothing available in your area which you feel meets your needs, you might want to consider starting a co-operative yourself. Preschools are particularly popular for parents and there are several support groups and resources available on the internet if you are interested. Creating the right kind of learning environment for the optimal development of social character and academic achievement requires reciprocity between the teachers, the children, and the parents.

Self-Education (autodidactic)

Self-education is not and has never been limited to school age children. Every person must learn and grow constantly throughout their lives, every stage of life from childhood, to adulthood, to parenthood, to grand-parenthood, through new jobs, experiences and challenges all provide learning. No one should ever fear the concept of education or doubt their capacity to learn. The internet and extraordinary initiatives such as open-source software, peer to peer universities and other resources, such as workshops, on-the-job-training, and books are some of the most marvelous tools in helping people to explore themselves, the universe, their place in it and expanding their minds and their outlooks.

A good book can not only take you on adventures, but it can change your vision and perception of the world, the priorities that you have and the world you live in. There is too great an emphasis on qualifications within society, yet that institutionalized convention of measuring capacity does not measure worth and value. Sources of knowledge are all around you (not the least of which are our elders) and in our own capacities to explore, observe, intuit and reason. Having faith in your own capacity and dedicating yourself to cultivating your own mind and exploring new ideas, will help you to understand your child's capacity, to set them a positive example and to have faith that they have the capacity to find their own passion and contribution to the world. Believe in yourself and believe in your child. No one could ever have taught you all that you have learned, just as no one is teaching your child to walk, and talk, and be kind and generous.

"In the end, the secret to learning is so simple: forget about it. Think only about whatever you love. Follow it, do it, dream it. One day, you will glance up at your collection of Japanese literature, or trip over the solar oven you built, and it will hit you: learning was there all the time, happening by itself." **Grace Llewellyn**

Children are already perfect, already good enough, we can only hope to preserve their natural capacities and aid them by providing the basic tools that they need to discover this wondrous world and this miracle that is life, with self-confidence, self-awareness, and self-discipline.

"Man is born to live and not to prepare to live." **Boris Pasternak**

Conclusion

"...if we continue replicating models of hierarchy and control in our schools, our youth will continue to replicate these systems as they exit the schools and enter the world. If we want a society that holds values such as mutual aid, respect, and cooperation, then these need to be the basis of our education system." **Co-operative Principles Can Be Applied in School Settings** *by Kiran Nigam* http://geo.coop/node/439

While there are many ways to raise and educate your children, it is important to recognize that your children came to you, because you are exactly the right parents for them for this life. You will provide them with the conditions in which to find and fulfill their unique purpose in this life. Learning is a constant and continuous part of life, and an integral part of our being like breathing. Where there is true love and appreciation of learning and where natural curiosity is nurtured, there will be no resistance from the child, inspiration will flow harmoniously, motivating the child from within.

If you want to do the best for your children, then focus on embodying within yourself and within your own daily routine those characteristics and attributes which you want them to emulate. Most of us learn best when we are fully absorbed in a subject, surrounded by it on a regular basis and actively participating, so involve your children in your vocation, your hobbies and your day to day chores. The earlier they learn to master these tasks the more effortless it will be for them as they grow up.

Raise your children with love, to love and to live in love.

Blessings

Resources

Montessori UK
http://www.montessorieducationuk.org/

International Association for Steiner/Waldorf Early Childhood Education

Documentary film "The Finland Phenomenon" by Sean Faust

Waikato Waldorf School... developing the whole child What is Waldorf Education?

What Every Parent Should Know About Steiner-Waldorf Schools – the quackometer blog.

Kiran Nigam (2010). Co-operative principles can be applied in school settings, Grassroots Economic Organizing (GEO) Newsletter, Volume II, Issue 5, http://www.geo.coop/node/439

What is (and isn't) a democratic school? By Den Demokratiske skole

Tlf. 41415736

E-mail demoskole@gmail.com

www.dendemokratiskeskole.dk

Deschooling Society by Ivan Illich

About the Author

Mrs. Jemmais Keval-Baxter resides in Chile with her family. She is a Natural Childbirth Coach, Doula, Doula Trainer, Writer, and EFT Coach. For more information about her books and workshops, please consult her website at **www.hooponoponodoula.com**.

Did you enjoy this book?

Would you like to read more from

Jemmais Keval-Baxter

The Ho'oponopono Doula™?

Visit: www.hooponoponodoula.com and sign up for the mailing list to receive a Free E-books and find out more information about workshops, books, and events.

Other books in the series include:

A Doulas Guide to Nutrition

A Doulas Guide to The Placenta

A Doulas Guide to Breastfeeding

A Doulas Guide to Menstruation

Also by Jemmais Keval-Baxter Ho'oponopono Birth: Meditations on Ho'oponopono for Pregnancy and Childbirth

If you liked this book, please leave a review so that others can find it too.

www.ingramcontent.com/pod-product-compliance
Lightning Source LLC
Chambersburg PA
CBHW060712030426
42337CB00017B/2843